Tomasz J. Kopański

# Barbarossa Victims vol. 1

STRATUS

Published in Poland in 2025
by Wydawnictwo Stratus sp.j.
Żeromskiego 6A,
27-600 Sandomierz, Poland
e-mail: office@wydawnictwostratus.pl

as
MMPBooks
e-mail: office@mmpbooks.biz

© Wydawnictwo Stratus sp.j.
© 2025 MMPBooks
© Tomasz J. Kopański

www.mmpbooks.biz
www.wydawnictwostratus.pl

**ISBN: 978-83-67227-86-5**

*Editor in chief*
**Roger Wallsgrove**

*Editorial Team*
**Robert Pęczkowski**
**Artur Juszczak**

*Cover concept*
**Dariusz Grzywacz**

*Book layout concept*
**Dariusz Grzywacz**

**All photos: author's collection except stated**

*DTP*
**Wydawnictwo Stratus sp.j.**

**PRINTED IN POLAND**

# Foreword.

At dawn on 22 June 1941, German forces launched an attack along a vast front stretching from the Baltic Sea to the Carpathian Mountains against their "best ally" – Stalinist Russia. The element of surprise, combined with the concentration of powerful formations, primarily consisting of armoured and Motorized units supported by the air force, allowed the Germans to penetrate deep into Soviet territory. By early September 1941, they had reached the outskirts of Leningrad, captured Kyiv in the south, and by October threatened the capital of the Red Empire – Moscow.

The first stage of the war in Russia was marked by significant successes for the German *Luftwaffe*, which, as in previous campaigns, aimed to first crush the enemy's air forces. On 22 June at 3:15 am, selected crews from KG 2, KG 3, and KG 53 attacked 31 airfields where Soviet fighter units were stationed. Shortly afterward, another wave of several hundred bombers and fighters struck Russian airfields. In total, the Germans attacked 66 airfields – 11 in the Baltic District, 25 in the Western District, 24 in the Kyiv District, and 6 in the Odesa District. Some of these airfields were attacked multiple times. *Luftwaffe* pilots, facing little opposition, strafed and bombed the enemy aircraft lined up in long rows, like at a parade, with thousands of SD-2 fragmentation bombs.

By the end of the day, fighter pilots from JG 53 reported 74 kills and 28 aircraft destroyed on the ground, JG 51 pilots claimed 69 kills and 129 aircraft destroyed on the ground, while JG 54 pilots reported 45 kills and 35 aircraft destroyed. The crews of the Zerstörers and bombers also had reasons to be satisfied. For example, Me 110-equipped SKG 210, in 13 attacks on 14 airfields, destroyed 344 machines on the ground and a further 8 in the air. A lone Ju 88 from 3./KG 3 Blitz, piloted by Lt. Ihrig, massacred the Russian 39th SBAP stationed in Pinsk. The bomber crew claimed the destruction of 60 enemy aircraft, and the Russians later confirmed the loss of 43 SBs and 5 Pe-2s. In Kurowice near Lviv, Ju 88s from KG 51 destroyed 34 I-153 aircraft from the 66th ShAP, in Brest Me 109s set fire to 65 I-16s belonging to the 122nd IAP, and in Grodno, they destroyed a further 41 I-16s and 5 I-153s from the 33rd IAP.

The largest losses were suffered by the air units of the Western Special Military District. According to Russian data, the 9th SAD lost 347 out of 440 aircraft, the 10th SAD saw 188 of its 239 aircraft destroyed, and the 11th SAD lost 127 out of 199 planes. The 43rd IAD also lost the majority of its aircraft. By the end of the day, German pilots reported the destruction of 1,811 enemy aircraft, including 322 in aerial combat. German losses amounted to 61 aircraft, with an additional 11 lost by Romanian units fighting on the southern front. These figures are entirely credible. The Russians, known for their tendency to underreport losses and exaggerate victories (for example, Soviet fighter claims throughout the entire war are at least six times inflated!), admitted to losing as many as 1,200 aircraft by noon on 22 June, including 336 in aerial combat.

This raises the question of why the Soviets were so caught off guard and why they suffered such colossal losses in the early days of the war. It seems that there were several reasons for this turn of events. In 1939–1940, after signing an agreement with Germany, the "peace-loving USSR" seized significant areas of Central and Eastern Europe: in September 1939, most of Poland's territory (51% of its area), in March 1940, following the so-called Winter War, the southern part of Finland, and in June of that year, all of Lithuania, Latvia, and Estonia, as well as Northern Bukovina and Bessarabia, which belonged to Romania.

After this shift in borders, the Soviets began relocating numerous military units, including air force units, to the newly acquired territories. It appears that Stalin, who had 21,000 aircraft and 23,000 tanks at his disposal, was already planning to attack Germany. Consequently, many newly constructed airfields (a total of 251 facilities were either built or upgraded) were positioned right near the new border – sometimes even within the range of their "ally's" artillery fire.

The outbreak of war came at the most disadvantageous moment for the Soviets. They had not yet completed the concentration of troops along their western border, and the air force had only just begun re-equipping with new types of aircraft.

In 1940, the Russian aviation industry produced 10,565 aircraft, but only 86 of the new types (64 Yak-1s, 20 MiG-3s, and 2 Pe-2s). Another significant batch of new aircraft was delivered to the air force by the factories only in March 1941), and these began to reach the units in April and May.

The morning of 22 June 1941. Extraordinary photographs capture the moment of the attack on a Soviet airfield used by a unit equipped with I-153 fighters. In the first photograph, we see an I-153 aircraft with its fuselage and engine still covered by a protective cover, while in the second, SD-2 fragmentation bombs can be seen, which caused devastating damage among the parked aircraft.

After the attack – on a captured Russian airfield. A destroyed I-153 fighter lies in the foreground, and in the background, there is a Bf 109E, possibly from JG 77. Under the fuselage of the Messerschmitt, a pylon carrying 96 SD-2 fragmentation bombs can be seen, which were used only in the early days of the war in Russia.

Another airfield, littered with the wreckage of MiG-3, Yak-4, and I-153 aircraft.

The remains of Russian aircraft destroyed on the airfield by SD-2 bombs. Fighters lined up in neat rows – here, MiG-1 and I-16 – became easy targets for the German pilots.

The aircraft that were introduced into service, however, had numerous defects, particularly the MiG-1/3 fighters, and by the time the war broke out, only a small portion of the flying personnel had been trained on them. As a result, at the time of the German attack, many airfields in the western part of the Soviet Union, where the new types of aircraft were primarily directed, housed a massive number of planes. In most regiments, the older aircraft were retained until the personnel were fully trained on the new types. This mass of aircraft occupied most of the available space on the airfield edges, making them easy targets for enemy bombs.

These bombs began to fall on the completely unsuspecting Russian troops at dawn on 22 June 1941. The blame for this undoubtedly lies with Stalin, who, until the very end, refused to acknowledge the numerous reports warning of a German attack. Weakened by the loss of many experienced pilots, who had fallen victim to Stalin's "purges", the Soviet air force was forced to engage in combat. At least on paper, it was an enormous force, with 61 air divisions and over 21,000 aircraft (13,288 belonging to the ground forces, 2,311 to the air defence forces, 1,452 to the navy, and 3,934 in aviation schools), of which over 10,000 were stationed in the western part of the country.

On the very first day of the war, it became evident that the German *Luftflotte* 1, 2, and 4, with fewer than 3,000 aircraft, had managed to achieve total air supremacy. The decisive factor was, of course, the element of surprise and the destruction of a large number of Russian aircraft on the ground. However, by the end of the first day, the Soviets still had over 8,000 aircraft in the western part of the country – nearly three times more than the attacking *Luftwaffe*. This situation once again demonstrated that success depends on many factors, not just numerical superiority. The *Luftwaffe* outperformed the Soviet air force in almost every aspect.

A significant problem for the Soviet air force was the lack of unified command and its division into various command structures: the Main Command (DBA – 13.5% of the forces stationed in the western part of the country), military district commands (40.5% of the forces), army commands (43.5%), corps commands (2.3% of the aircraft), and independent naval aviation. This fragmentation made coordination extremely difficult for the Soviets and contributed to their enormous losses.

Technical superiority also played a major role in the German success. The German aircraft were generally more modern, faster, better armed, and better equipped. This superiority allowed them to choose the time and manner of engagement. In contrast, Soviet aircraft were equipped with only the most basic onboard instruments, and radios were a rarity, particularly in fighters. Theoretically, every fifteenth aircraft, usually reserved for squadron or regiment commanders, was equipped with a radio, but, for example, none of the first thousand Yak-1s had radios. This made group flights exceedingly difficult, and during aerial combat, the lack of communication led to additional losses.

It is also important to highlight that many Soviet pilots were deployed to combat units after having flown solo for only 8–10 hours (!), which meant they posed little threat to the experienced *Luftwaffe* crews. In aviation schools, they were not taught how to conduct normal, manoeuvrable aerial combat, nor were they trained to fly in difficult weather conditions or without visible landmarks.

As a result, Soviet losses increased rapidly. On 23 June, the Germans destroyed 755 enemy aircraft, on 24 June – 557, on 25 June – 251, on 26 June – 300, and by 1 July, they had eliminated a total of 4,725 Soviet planes. Of these, 1,392 were shot down in aerial combat, 112 were downed by Flak, and 3,221 were destroyed on the ground.

A significant portion of the downed aircraft were SB bombers from the ground forces' aviation, as well as DB-3/DB-3F bombers from Long-Range Aviation, which were the easiest targets for the Germans. For instance, JG 51 pilots reported shooting down 57 SB bombers on 24 June, 68 SB bombers on 25 June, 40 DB-3 bombers on 26 June, and 113 aircraft, mainly bombers, on 30 June. On 15 July 1941, the commander of JG 51, Oberst Werner Mölders, became the first pilot in World War II to achieve his 100th and 101st aerial victories.

The massacre of bombers was, in part, facilitated by the Soviets themselves. They sent these bombers on desperate missions to attack the advancing German armoured and Motorized columns, as well as bridge crossings, without any fighter escort. As a result, Soviet airmen paid the ultimate price for the lack of coordinated operations, which – as is well known – was a consequence of a flawed command system. Bombers under the command of military district headquarters (later, fronts) had to operate independently because most fighter units were under the control of different commanders – those of the armies.

Throughout the summer and autumn of 1941, the Soviets continued to suffer heavy losses. By 30 September, the Germans claimed to have destroyed 14,500 aircraft, including 5,000 in aerial combat. By the end of the year, this number had exceeded 20,000. The Soviets themselves officially admitted to losing 20,159 aircraft during this period, including 16,620 combat aircraft.

The Russian ground forces also suffered enormous losses. By 30 September, they had lost 20,500 tanks, 101,000 guns and mortars, and millions of soldiers. By the end of the year, it is estimated that the human losses reached 2.663 million killed in action and 3.350 million taken prisoner. During the same period, German losses were twenty times smaller.

Despite the heavy blows dealt to the Red Army in 1941, contrary to German hopes, it did not collapse. Russian soldiers feared their commanders and the infamous NKVD more than the enemy. Reprisals against those deemed responsible for the defeats of the summer of 1941 also affected the air force. Almost all the commanders of the air districts paid with their positions, and in some cases, with their lives. Additionally, pilots who returned from combat missions with unused ammunition had little chance of surviving to the next day. This was how Stalin "motivated" his soldiers to fight.

At the same time, numerous arms factories were producing large quantities of various equipment. Through enormous effort and the use of even women and children in forced labour, the Soviets managed to produce 5,600 new tanks and 7,900 aircraft by the end of 1941. This allowed them to partially replenish the massive losses, although the equipment produced under such difficult conditions and by unskilled workers, often using substitute materials, was of significantly lower quality than that produced before the war.

The impressive successes that the Germans achieved in Russia did not come easily. By 6 December 1941, the *Luftwaffe* units fighting on the Eastern Front had lost no fewer than 2,093 aircraft, including 758 bombers, 586 fighters, and 170 dive bombers. An additional 1,362 aircraft were damaged.

In the following years of the war, it became clear that the Eastern Front was the most exhausting and costly area of operations for the Germans, and that the Russians, thanks to their mobilization and production capabilities, played a significant role in the eventual defeat of Germany.

In the first weeks and months of the war in Russia, the Germans not only destroyed a vast number of enemy aircraft but also captured hundreds of functional or slightly damaged planes abandoned by the Soviets. However, only a small number of these were later used as training aircraft in schools (e.g., UTI-4) or as liaison aircraft within units.

Despite expressed interest from Japan and Iraq in acquiring the captured Soviet I-16 and UTI-4 aircraft, these sales did not materialize. The reasons were either transportation difficulties (Japan) or the subsequent presence of British forces in Iraq. As a result, only Finland received a dozen or so aircraft of various types, while the remaining stored aircraft gradually deteriorated.

# Glossary

| | | |
|---|---|---|
| AA | *Armieyskaya Aviatsiya* | – Army Aviation |
| AD | *Aviatsionnaya Diviziya* | – Aviation Division |
| AE | *Aviatsionnaya Eskadrilya* | – Aviation Squadron |
| BAB | *Bombardirovochnaya Aviatsionnaya Brigada* | – Bomber Aviation Brigade |
| BAD | *Bombardirovochnaya Aviatsionnaya Diviziya* | – Bomber Aviation Division |
| BAK | *Bombardirovochniy Aviatsionniy Korpus* | – Bomber Aviation Corps |
| BAP | *Bombardirovochniy Aviatsionniy Polk* | – Bomber Aviation Regiment |
| BBAP | *Blizhnebombardirovochniy Aviatsionniy Polk* | – Short Range Bomber Aviation Regiment |
| DBA | *Dal'ne Bombardirovochnaya Aviatsiya* | – Long Range Bomber Aviation |
| DBAD | *Dal'ne Bombardirovochnaya Aviatsionnaya Diviziya* | – Long Range Bomber Aviation Division |
| DBAP | *Dal'ny Bombardirovochniy Aviatsionniy Polk* | – Long Range Bomber Aviation Regiment |
| FA | *Frontovaya Aviatsiya* | – Front Aviation: Aviation of military districts |
| IAB | *Istriebitel'naya Aviatsionnaya Brigada* | – Fighter Aviation Brigade |
| IAD | *Istriebitel'naya Aviatsionnaya Diviziya* | – Fighter Aviation Division |
| IAP | *Istriebitel'niy Aviatsionniy Polk* | – Fighter Aviation Regiment |
| JG | *Jagdgeschwader* | – Fighter Group |
| KAE | *Korpusnaya Aviatsionnaya Eskadrilya* | – Aviation Squadron of the Ground Army Corps |
| KG | *Kampfgeschwader* | – Bomber Group |
| MTAP | *Minno-Torpedniy Aviatsionniy Polk* | – Torpedo Aviation Regiment |
| OMRAP | *Otdielniy Morskoy Razvedyvatelniy Aviatsionniy Polk* | – Independet Naval Reconnaissance Aviation Regiment |
| ORAE | *Otdielnaya Razvedyvatelnaya Aviatsionnaya Eskadrilya* | – Independet Naval Reconnaissance Aviation Squadron |
| PVO | *Protivo-Vozdushnaya Oborona* | – Home Air Defece |
| RAP | *Razvedyvatelniy Aviatsionniy Polk* | – Reconnaissance Aviation Regiment |
| SAB | *Smieshannaya Aviatsionnaya Brigada* | – Composite Aviation Brigade |
| SAD | *Smieshannaya Aviatsionnaya Diviziya* | – Composite Aviation Division |
| SAP | *Smieshanniy Aviatsionniy Polk* | – Composite Aviation Regiment |
| SBAP | *Skorostnoy Bombardirovochniy Aviatsionniy Polk* | – High-speed Bomber Aviation Regiment |
| ShAP | *Shturmovoy Aviatsionniy Polk* | – Ground Attack Aviation Regiment |
| TBAP | *Tyazhyeliy Bombardirovochniy Aviatsionniy Polk* | – Heavy Bomber Aviation Regiment |
| VMF | *Voyenno Morskoy Flot* | – The Navy |
| VVS | *Voyenno Vozdushnye Sily* | – Military Air Force |

# Gloster Gladiator

A group of five ex-Latvian Gloster Gladiator Mk I aircraft, which were seized by the Germans at the Krustpils airfield in the summer of 1941. The damaged aircraft in the foreground bears the insignia of one of the two Latvian squadrons equipped with this type and a Latvian registration number, most likely "168." All Latvian Gladiators (26 in total) were purchased in England in 1937. They bore the numbers 114–126 and 163–175.

Another group of ex-Latvian Gladiators, which were used by the Russians. Notably, the aircraft "116" displays the Latvian squadron insignia, alongside the new owner's markings placed over the painted-over Latvian red swastika. This change occurred after the Soviet invasion of the Baltic states on 17 June 1940, when they seized their armaments. A year later, following the German attack, some of the Latvian and Lithuanian aircraft were destroyed, but the Germans captured 11 Gladiators in good condition (mainly Latvian) and 2 more that were seriously damaged. The *Luftwaffe* later used these aircraft as tow planes for DFS 230 gliders in the training unit Erg. Gr (S)1 at Langendiebach near Hanau.

# Polikarpov I-15, I-15bis

A captured Polikarpov I-5 by the Germans, marked with a white number "6" on the tail. Between 1931 and 1934, the Russians built 803 fighters of this type. As of early 1939, 89 of these aircraft were still in service, and several dozen survived until the German invasion in 1941. After being equipped with two bomb racks under the fuselage (as seen in the photo), they were used as light ground-attack aircraft. As of 1 September 1941, the 11th ShAP, operating near Sevastopol, still had 20 of these aircraft in service.

Photographed by the Germans, likely in southern Russia, is the wreckage of an I-5 fighter. In the rear section of the fuselage, a three-colour camouflage pattern and a fragment of a red star are clearly visible. Factory-new aircraft of this type could reach speeds of 252 km/h at an altitude of 5,000 meters and 278 km/h at ground level. By 1941, these planes were already considered relics of the past.

The I-15 bis (I-152) aircraft, abandoned by the Soviets at one of the airfields, was just as outdated as the I-5. At the outbreak of war with Germany, it was still in service with ten fighter regiments across five border military districts, totaling 268 aircraft (including 27 unserviceable). An additional 145 aircraft were in naval aviation, including 29 with the Baltic Fleet.

Photographed by the Germans, likely in southern Russia, is the wreckage of an I-5 fighter. In the rear section of the fuselage, a three-colour camouflage pattern and a fragment of a red star are clearly visible. Factory-new aircraft of this type could reach speeds of 252 km/h at an altitude of 5,000 meters and 278 km/h at ground level. By 1941, these planes were already considered relics of the past.

A similar aircraft, still equipped with its propeller spinner. These fighters, fitted with racks for four 25 or 32 kg bombs, were most often used for ground attack missions.

The same aircraft as in the previous photo, but now more severely damaged. Noteworthy is the camouflage on the interwing struts, likely applied with green paint up to about half their height.

A burned-out wreck of an I-15 bis at an airfield in Kaunas. The aircraft features an unusual paint scheme – a dark colour around the entire front section of the engine cowling and spinner, likely in the squadron's colour. In the background, there is a Bf 109 F from the II Gruppe of a German *Luftwaffe* unit.

A German soldier inspects the cockpit equipment of the I-15 bis.

The "belly" section of an I-15 bis shot down by the Germans.

The airfield in Vilnius after being captured by the Germans. The photo shows, among other things, an SB bomber in the background, an I-153 in the centre, and an I-15 bis on the right. The aircraft has aerodynamic wheel covers but is missing its red stars, which German soldiers often cut out to take as souvenirs.

# Polikarpov I-153

The airfield in Barysaw was spotted with an I-153 bearing the number 3 stripped of its fabric covering by its captors. This aircraft is somewhat unusual, as it was equipped with a radio installation (the mast is visible on the right upper wing). The aircraft was also armed with RS-82 rocket launchers (four under each lower wing), which were intended to enhance its effectiveness in ground-attack missions.

"Souvenir from Russia": Another I-153 "Chaika" equipped with a radio and also bearing the tactical number "3". However, this particular aircraft does not have the RS-82 rocket rails under the wings, but rather bomb racks.

Pair of Light Grey (?) Wrecks: A pair of I-153 wrecks in one of the Soviet air bases. The aircraft on the left has the older type of spinner, borrowed from the I-15 bis, while the one on the right features the newer design. It's noteworthy that even the propellers were painted with the same colour as the fuselages.

The I-153 with a very unusual paint scheme resulting from damage repairs. The central part of the fuselage appears whitish (which is why Germans sometimes described such aircraft as having a winter camouflage), while the upper wings and rear fuselage are silver or light grey. The whitish strips are fabric tapes applied over joints or bullet holes. On the rudder, a yellow number "7" with a black outline is visible, and in front of it, an illegible serial number.

An identically painted and similarly treated I-153 by the enemy. This aircraft is also two-toned – the fuselage is lighter, while the wings, horizontal stabilizers, and rudder are darker. The dark and light stripes are fabric tapes (whitish in colour, which should have been painted over with special lacquer after application) glued over the damaged areas.

A captured I-153 in Lviv with bomb racks under the wings. This aircraft had also undergone repairs (visible on the upper part of the strut) and was subsequently stripped of its fabric covering by the Germans, allowing a clear view of the fuselage's lattice structure.

An I-153 with damaged covering on the left wings. This aircraft also shows signs of repainting on the rear fuselage and vertical stabilizer. The rudder bears the number "10" likely in red.

A similar gathering of captured I-153s, this time at the Polish airfield in Vilnius, on 2 July 1941. On the right and left are aircraft in green camouflage, in the middle a silver one with a light grey rudder, and just behind it, a light grey one with dark elements; all the "Chaikas" bear tactical numbers (2, 3, 13, 12). On the left, we see an R-5, and behind it, a U-2.

A light grey I-153 with the number "6" and four bomb racks for 200 kg bombs at the airfield in Olita (Alytus), Lithuania. This aircraft belonged to the 42ⁿᵈ IAP and remained in excellent condition, which was rare at the time.

A group of differently painted I-153s illustrates perfectly the varied colour schemes of the VVS (Soviet Air Force) at that time: on the right, a light grey machine; in the centre, a dark green/light blue one; and on the left, a silver aircraft with an irregular brush-applied camouflage pattern.

A silver I-153 captured by the Germans, possibly somewhere in Lithuania. The aircraft, featuring red (or possibly blue?) markings on the vertical stabilizer and rudder, is clearly visible in both photographs. These images are worth studying as they contribute to the discussion on the interpretation of colours in black-and-white photographs.

A silver I-153 with the number 52 (indicating continuity in numbering throughout the regiment) abandoned by the Soviets.

An I-153, as usual, with a tactical number on the rudder (unfortunately illegible). The I-153 was the last mass-produced fighter designed by Polikarpov. Armed with 4 machine guns, it could reach a speed of just over 400 km/h.

The wreckage of the I-153 reveals the structural details of this aircraft: the wing ribs, the fuel tank, and the fuselage's framework.

A similar shot, once again showcasing the details of the fuselage and the lower surfaces of the aircraft, including the landing gear bays and bomb racks. These bomb racks were installed to enhance the striking power of the Soviet VVS, as the I-153s were intended to function primarily as ground-attack aircraft, with their role as fighters being secondary.

A collection of fuselage frameworks from I-15bis and I-153 aircraft. Once again, it's worth paying attention to the structural details, particularly the horizontal stabilizers.

If an I-153 didn't have bomb racks, it was equipped with RS-82 rocket launchers. On this aircraft, due to the collapse of the landing gear and the subsequent nose-over, these launchers are clearly visible.

An I-153 with the number 15, not yet prepared for action, was abandoned at an airfield. On the right upper wing, we can see an antenna mast, a feature that was only present on command aircraft.

Another shot of an I-153 equipped with RS-82 rocket launchers, this time bearing the number 1. The fuselage was damaged by the pilot, but the tears in the fabric covering were caused by German souvenir hunters.

A whitish-silver (or light grey?) I-153 with the number 11, indicating it belonged to the 1st squadron of the regiment.

Two I-153 aircraft withdrawn from frontline service and stored at the side of an airfield. Both aircraft are equipped with bomb locks, and the one in the background is armed with RS-82 rocket launchers. The photo was almost certainly taken in Kėdainiai, Lithuania.

Another I-153 "Chaika" camouflaged at the edge of a grove. It is likely that the aircraft's previous tactical number was painted over and replaced with a new one – "3".

An I-153, likely damaged in combat, ended up on its nose during rollout after landing, in late June 1941. The paint scheme is typical for the VVS: red stars with black outlines and a circle in the centre on the fuselage and wings.

The same aircraft photographed slightly later from the other side. The tactical number is clearly visible, along with a hole in the tailplane that wasn't present in the previous photo. It's also worth noting the matte shade of the paint on the upper wings, which contrasts sharply with the finish on the fuselage. In the background, there is the wreckage of a MiG-3, and behind it, a Fi 156 Storch (possibly marked SI+P?) and a Ju 52.

An I-153, likely painted in light grey, with the tactical number "29". In Soviet units, a uniform numbering system was usually maintained for the entire regiment (from 1 to 65), sometimes using different colours for these numbers to distinguish between squadrons. The photo was most likely taken in Minsk, so the aircraft probably belonged to the 160th IAP, the only unit in the 43rd IAD equipped with I-153 "Chaikas".

In the background, you can see the same I-153 with the number "29." In the foreground, a *Luftwaffe* soldier stands by the wreckage of another I-153.

Photographed at the same airfield is an I-153 "Chaika" with a very interesting camouflage pattern. Dark green "squiggles" were brushed onto the silver background of the aircraft, except for the outer sections of the upper wings. The rudder bears the number "63" in a black outline, likely in red or yellow. The order to create such camouflage patterns in regiments was issued around mid-June 1941, but it was not implemented everywhere.

On the right is the same "Chaika" number "63". The left tip of the upper wing, without camouflage, is clearly visible, and in the background, there is a dark green I-16 with the number 3 on the rudder and stars on the upper wing surface.

Another shot of the same I-153, this time showing the camouflage pattern on the engine cowling. Bomb racks are visible under the left lower wing. In the foreground, the rudder of an I-16 with a white number "3" can be seen.

The Porubanek airbase near Vilnius (renamed by the Germans as Wilno-South) shortly after its capture by *Luftflotte* 1 units. In the foreground, there is a silver I-153 with the number 10, although the red stars have been removed, and behind it, an I-16 Type 5, which by the summer of 1941 was primarily used only for operational training. In the background, there is a Me 110, likely from ZG 26.

The owner of this "Chaika" left the aircraft under good protection. However, this did not prevent the Germans from capturing the machine.

An I-153, likely in an unusable condition, captured at the airfield in Orsha.

Some of these "Chaikas" could likely have been restored to operational status if not for the activities of souvenir hunters, who stripped the aircraft of parts of their covering.

A captured light grey I-153 with clearly visible bomb racks under the wings.

# Polikarpov I-16

A base cluttered with the wreckage of VVS aircraft. The I-16 on the right is the UTI-4 trainer version, a relatively rare sight in photographs despite being produced in over 3,180 units. In the centre is an I-16 Type 6, with an I-15 bis behind it. On the left, remnants of a MiG-3 can be seen.

A UTI-4 captured by the Germans in perfect condition. This is an early model with fixed landing gear and old-style windscreens. Some early-ly-series UTI-4s were equipped with one-piece front windscreens, which later became standard.

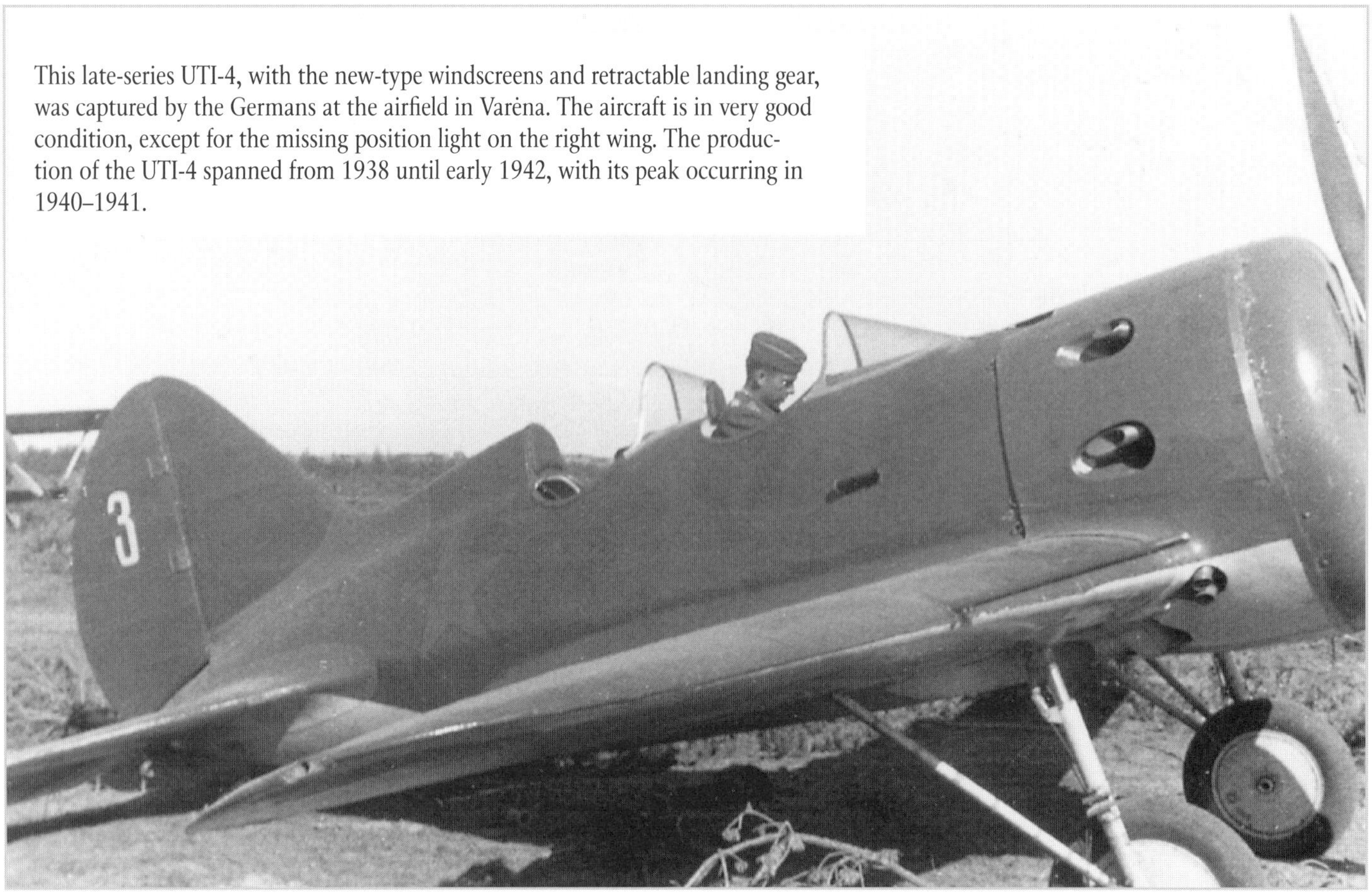

This late-series UTI-4, with the new-type windscreens and retractable landing gear, was captured by the Germans at the airfield in Varėna. The aircraft is in very good condition, except for the missing position light on the right wing. The production of the UTI-4 spanned from 1938 until early 1942, with its peak occurring in 1940–1941.

The pilot of this UTI-4 made an emergency landing on the roof of a rural house in Demidov. As a result, both the house and the aircraft were destroyed. A white stripe is visible on the left wing of the aircraft, which could indicate that the plane was very worn out and not suitable for aerobatics. Such a stripe was usually painted on the fuselage, behind the instructor's cockpit. However, the missing part of the aircraft does not allow us to determine definitively whether the stripe was painted on this specific example. The photograph was taken by a German soldier in September 1941.

As you can see, no difficulties could deter the German soldiers from doing their laundry. It's worth noting the details of the UTI-4, especially the windscreens and the inscription "brat' zdjes" (take here) in front of the horizontal stabilizer. On the elevator, you can also see a number that can be read as 1815423.

A UTI-4 abandoned by the Soviets in Olita, Lithuania. The different colouring of the aircraft's nose is noticeable, likely due to the use of different varnishes and the mixed construction of the aircraft (wooden fuselage, fabric-covered stabilizers, and a metal engine cowling). This is a later model with retractable landing gear, but it has the old-style windscreen for the instructor's cockpit.

Another pair of UTI-4s captured by the Germans in early August 1941. It's worth noting that the aircraft differ in the shade of paint on their upper surfaces, but this is likely due to different lighting conditions rather than the use of different paints.

The same UTI-4 as on the adjacent page, seen from a 3/4 front view. It's worth noting the unusual placement of the stars on the lower surface of the wings (they were usually painted closer to the wingtips) and the different colouring of the engine cowling on its lower, right side.

A nearly promotional shot of an I-16 Type 5 at one of the bases used by the Germans. This version of the "Ishak" had an enclosed cockpit. The one-piece canopy slid forward on special rails. The armament consisted of only two ShKAS machine guns. Type 5 aircraft had not been produced since early 1939.

"Ishaks" stored in a hangar at one of the bases near Šiauliai in Lithuania: All the visible aircraft (at least four) are in perfect condition and could have been used by their captors. However, the Germans did not find this opportunity enticing.

**Below:** A line of I-16 Type 5 aircraft somewhere in the USSR. The machines have two-tone tactical numbers on the rudders, which indicates they were likely red or blue (both colours did not stand out much against the dark green background) with white outlines. The OP-1 gunsights were most likely removed by the Germans.

The wreckage of I-16 Type 5 aircraft reveals details of their construction

**Above & below:** Two views of the base area, likely where workshops were located, early July 1941. This area was used for repairing I-16s, I-153s, and even I-15 bis aircraft. In the upper photo, on the right, we can see the same "Ishak" as in the adjacent photo. It is a Type 5 with the number "1" (which appears to be a colour other than red).

The wreckage of an I-16 Type 5 with a very high and unusual tactical number "72." The photo clearly shows the engine frame and wing structure.

An I-16 shot down by the Germans, featuring unit markings on the rudder. This consists of an outline running along the edge of the rudder, separated from the camouflage by a white stripe. The number (likely "60") is also two-toned.

The same aircraft being inspected by German soldiers. This is an I-16 Type 10 – the first version to receive enhanced armament, consisting of 4 machine guns (2 in the wings and 2 above the engine).

An I-16, likely a Type 10, abandoned at one of the Soviet bases. The rudder features the number 6, likely in yellow or blue.

**Above:** Inspection of an I-16 Type 5 abandoned by the Soviets during transport to an airfield by land, mid-July 1941. The aircraft had been left for quite some time before being captured by the Germans, as evidenced by the dirt on the rear fuselage and horizontal stabilizers; the areas covered by a tarpaulin remained clean.

I-16 Type 5 aircraft abandoned by the Soviets at an airfield.

"Before Takeoff": A *Luftwaffe* soldier prepares for a souvenir photo in the cockpit of an I-16 Type 5.

Another I-16 Type 5 captured by the Germans. The aircraft still has its OP-1 gunsight. The Germans typically removed this component from captured aircraft, which effectively prevented their use in combat.

A demolished wreck of an I-16, stripped of its tires and camouflage paint on the wooden fuselage. The metal and fabric elements of the tail, however, still retain their dark green colour.

An I-16 Type 5 abandoned in Varėna. As is clearly visible, the Germans captured it in an intact condition.

A very unusually painted older-production I-16, likely a Type 6. The fighter is coated in silver paint on all surfaces, with black "decorations" visible around the engine cowling area. The tactical number, as always, is painted on the rudder.

An I-16 Type 5 abandoned in Varėna. As is clearly visible, the Germans captured it in an intact condition.

Another I-16 Type 5 abandoned on the roads of the Soviet retreat. This aircraft shows signs of light damage, as well as a tactical number (a "7" on the rudder) painted in a very unusual manner – using black paint.

A scrapyard in one of the Soviet bases, probably in Minsk. In the foreground are I-16 Type 27 aircraft, equipped with ShVAK 20 mm cannons in the wings and two ShKAS machine guns above the engine. These aircraft could have belonged to one of the fighter regiments of the 43rd IAD, namely the 161st, 162nd, or 163rd IAP. It appears that all of them have colourful tactical numbers painted on the stabilizers, as well as striking lightning bolts – likely a designation of affiliation with a specific regiment.

The same location photographed from the other side. The I-16 in the foreground shows clear signs of damage on the wing, which has been repaired with fabric patches. In the background, on the right, an I-16 with the number "8" is visible.

Once again, the same group of aircraft. In the back, we see the I-16 from the previous photo (likely with a red number "8" in a white outline), and in front of it, another I-16 with a white number "10".

Two photos show an I-16 Type 5 "8", likely captured by the Germans at the airfield in Mitava, Latvia. The prominently visible rails for the sliding canopy and the colourful tip of the vertical stabilizer are noteworthy. The exact colour of this element is uncertain, but it appears to have been either blue or, more likely, yellow.

An I-16 Type 5 with the number "1" and a colourful stabilizer, photographed in Šiauliai, Lithuania, after losing its landing gear. It's worth noting the wing structure, and particularly the aircraft in the background – besides an SB with the number "12," there is a Lithuanian Gladiator (just above the cockpit of the I-16), and further to the right, two Lithuanian Ansaldo A-120s (one of which is missing its engine).

A lineup of various I-16s from the same unit. In the first row, we see an I-16 Type 5, followed by an I-16 Type 10, and then a UTI-4. In the background, there are U-2s, SBs, and an I-153.

Two shots of an I-16 Type 5 with the number "2" and an SL-17 gun camera positioned just behind the pilot's headrest. In later versions, the PAU-22 gun camera was typically used. These photos were taken at the airfield in Šiauliai, summer 1941.

A photo showing another I-16 Type 5 from the same regiment, this time with the tactical number "9" painted in a darker colour.

In the foreground, the same I-16 number "9" is seen from the rear. In the background, there are an R-5 and an SB, likely from the 46th SBAP.

Airfield in Šiauliai, June 1941: On the right, there is a trio of I-16 Type 5s from 2–3 different squadrons of the same regiment. On the left, there is a MiG-3, with an SB behind it, and in the distance to the left, an Ar-2.

Close-up of an I-16 Type 10 featuring a very unusual camouflage pattern. The vast majority of photographs confirm that I-16s typically appeared in green-light blue paint schemes. However, this particular aircraft is silver, with green, irregular camouflage applied by brush in June. In the background, I-16s with arrows on the vertical stabilizers can be seen. This photograph was most likely taken in Minsk.

Two German soldiers stand next to an I-16, likely a Type 18 or 24, which has already been partially stripped of its stars (taken as souvenirs!). Both of these types had the same armament as the I-16 Type 10, with 4 machine guns. The only difference was the engine: the I-16 Type 18 was equipped with a Shvetsov M-62 engine with 1,000 HP, while the Type 24 had an M-63 engine with 1,100 HP.

Another souvenir photo, this time in front of an I-16 Type 6. The factory numbers painted on the tail (621528 or 821528) indicate that the aircraft had undergone a major overhaul.

A German soldier checks under the wing of this I-16 Type 5 to see if the star is still intact, likely intending to cut it out as a souvenir.

This I-16 Type 5 was marked with a white number "6" on the rudder.

An I-16 Type 6 abandoned after a forced landing at an airfield later used by the Germans. Apart from the red star on the fuselage, the aircraft had no other markings.

The pilot of this I-16 Type 6 also managed to make a forced landing. The hole in the fuselage is likely the result of the star being cut out along with the plywood.

**Below & opposite page:** An I-16 Type 29 with a yellow number "4," though without a star on the fuselage! The Type 29 was the final modification of the I-16, armed with 2 ShKAS machine guns above the engine and a Berezin UBS 12.7 mm machine gun mounted below it. As a result, the air intake was shifted to the left.

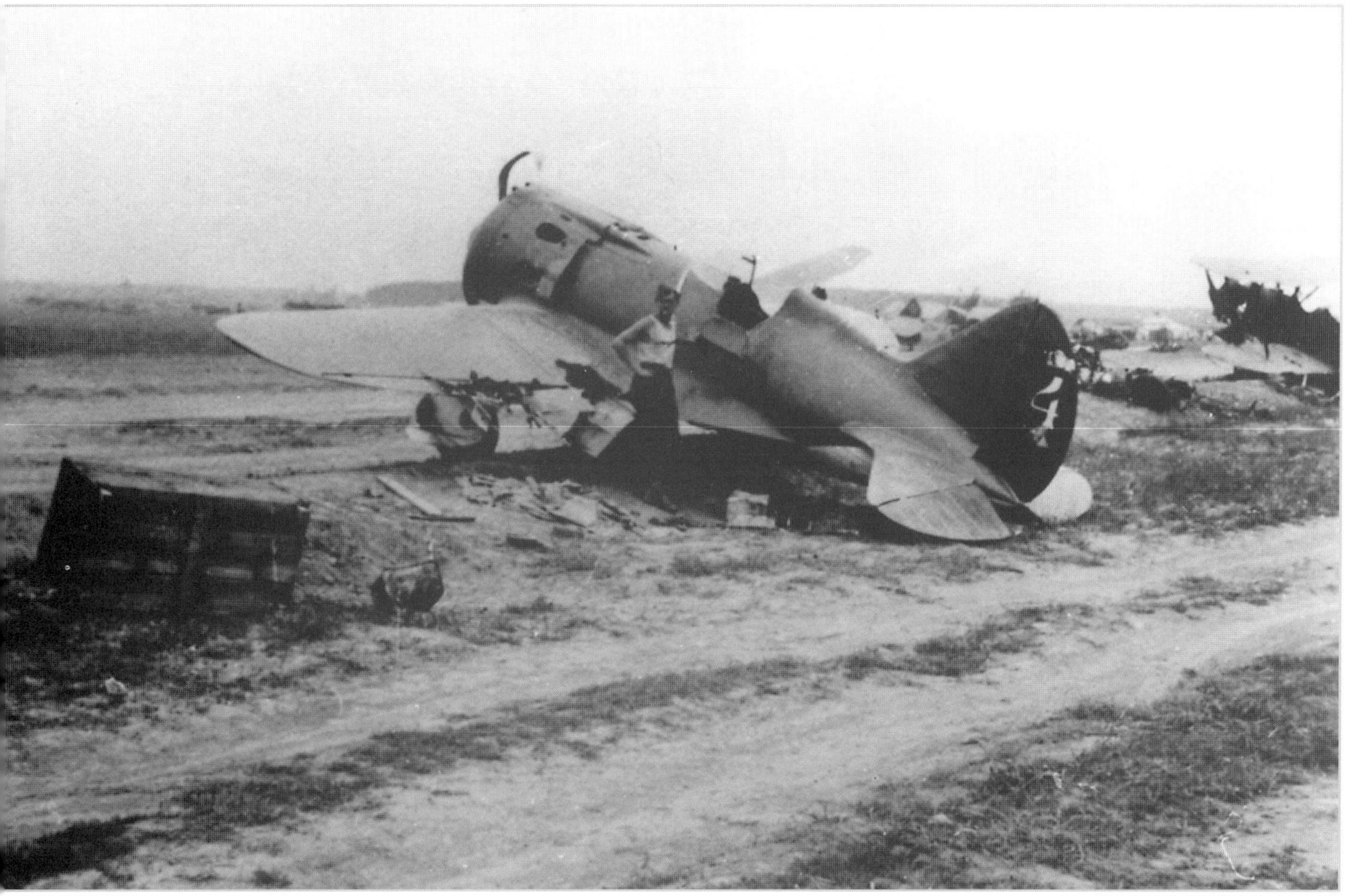

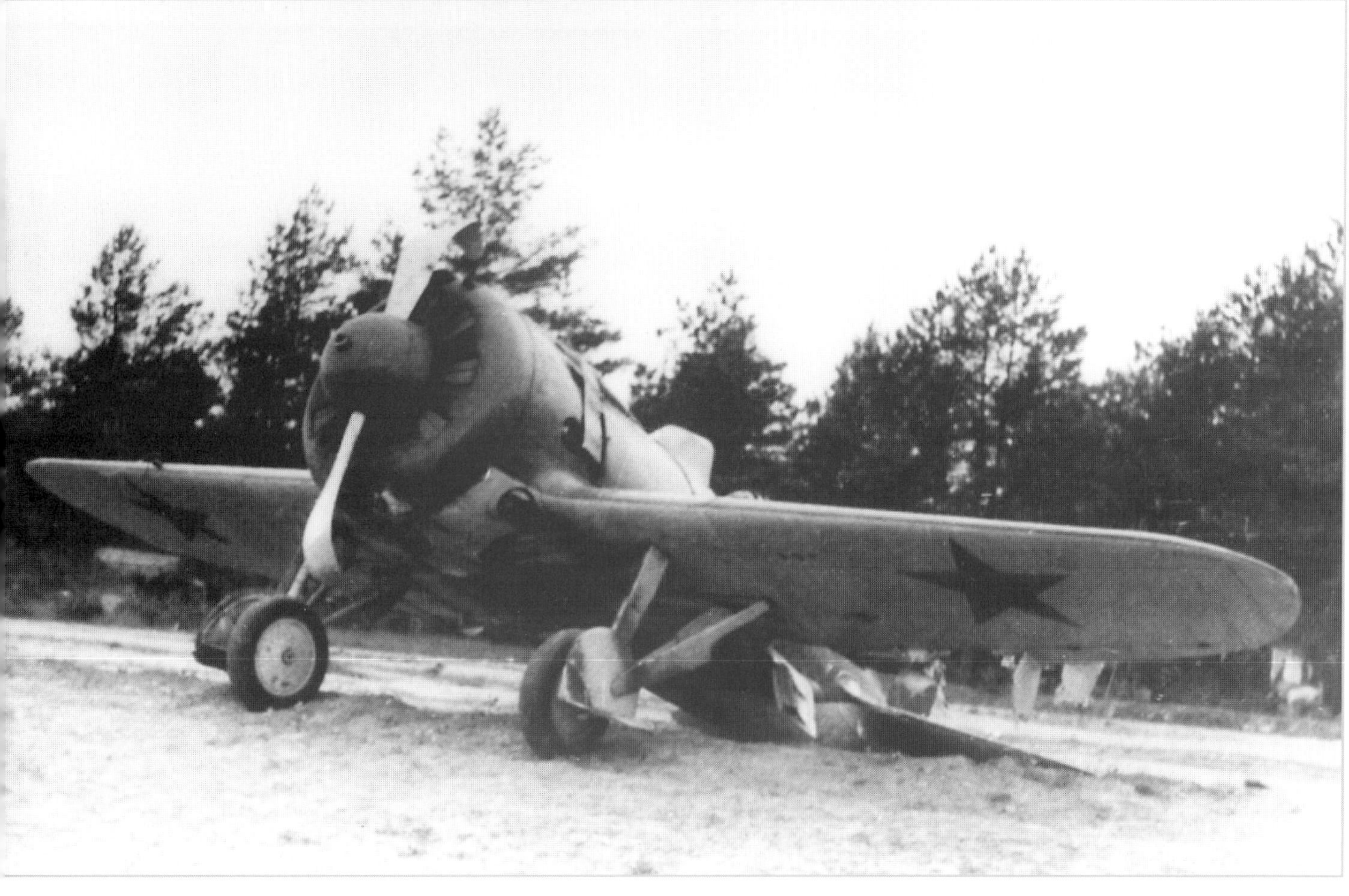

Another shot of a captured I-16 Type 29, this time marked with the number "15." Under the propeller spinner, the muzzle of the UBS machine gun is visible, and further to the left, the air intake. Aircraft in this version no longer had wing-mounted armament. The photographed example was equipped with a radio, with its antenna mast mounted on the right side of the engine cowling.

**Below**: German airmen at a field airfield. On the left lies an I-16 Type 29 marked with the number "6." In the centre is a damaged Hs-126, and on the right is a MiG-3.

This I-16 Type 29 has very unusual armament. In addition to its standard machine guns, it is equipped with a bomb rack and three RS-82 rocket rails under each wing.

A slightly damaged I-16 type 29 with the number "9" abandoned by the Soviets somewhere at the edge of a small forest. The aircraft was equipped with RS-82 rocket launchers and an RSI-3 radio. Its antenna mast is visible above the engine cowling.

# Mikoyan Gurevich MiG-3

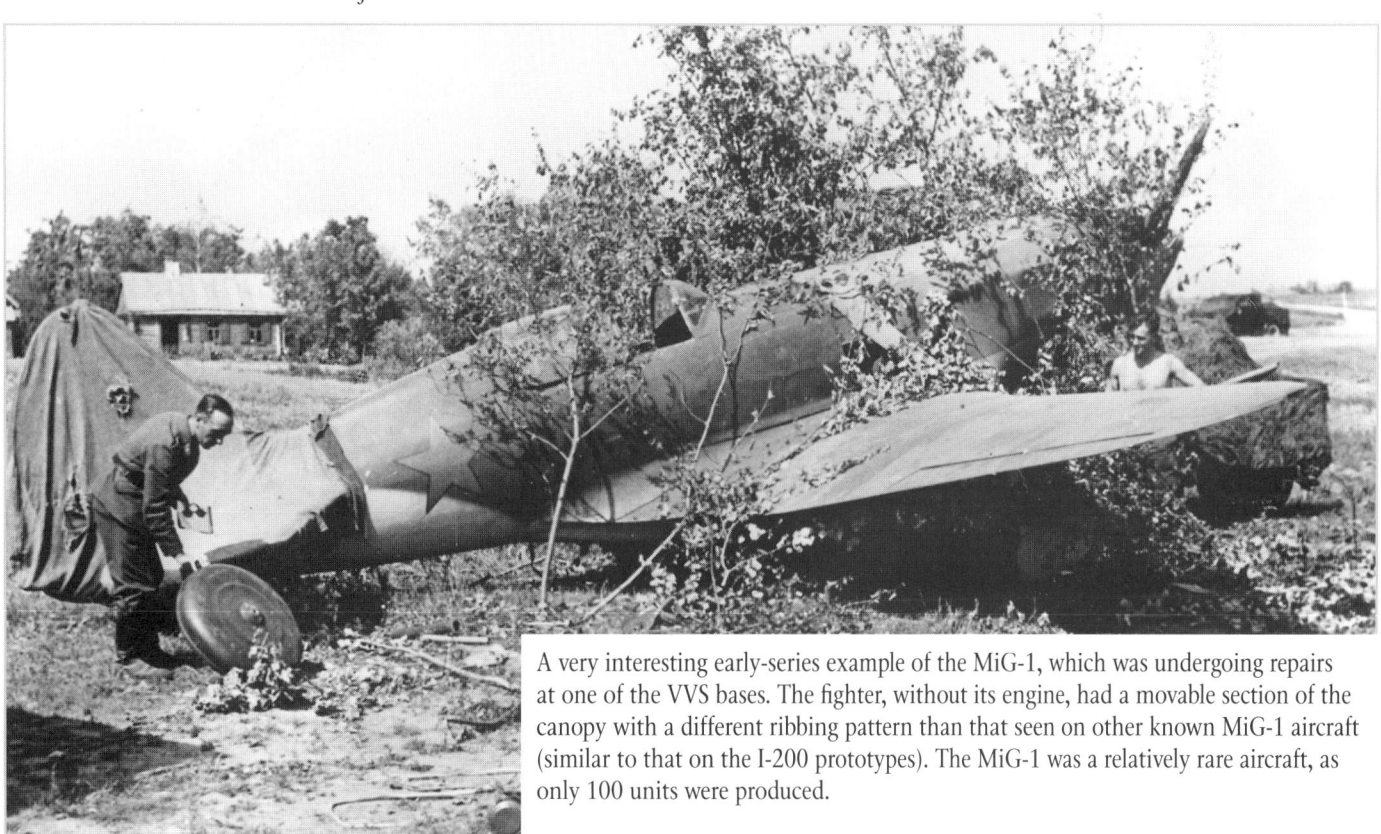

The photo shows a MiG-1 captured by the Germans. The aircraft was nearly identical to the MiG-3 fighter, which began production in January 1941, and externally differed only in the shape of the landing gear covers and a shorter radiator under the fuselage. In the background, there are an Ar-2 dive bomber and a Ju 88.

A very interesting early-series example of the MiG-1, which was undergoing repairs at one of the VVS bases. The fighter, without its engine, had a movable section of the canopy with a different ribbing pattern than that seen on other known MiG-1 aircraft (similar to that on the I-200 prototypes). The MiG-1 was a relatively rare aircraft, as only 100 units were produced.

The first MiG-1 aircraft were delivered at the beginning of 1941 to the 41st IAP stationed in Białystok and the 31st IAP in Kaunas. The photo shows an aircraft likely belonging to the 31st IAP, marked with the number "5" on the tail. In the background, there are MiG-3 and R-5 aircraft.

The next photo shows the same group of machines. On the left, the front part of the MiG-1 fuselage, number "5", with a damaged aileron is visible. Under the wing of the aircraft, the lower part of the landing gear cover with its characteristic shape for this type of aircraft can be seen.

The MiG-3 aircraft with landing gear covers featuring a distinctive broken lower edge. From January 1941, this machine replaced the MiG-1 in production. The fighter shown in the photo was captured by the Germans at the 8th SAD airfield in Alytus, Lithuania.

The MiG-3, marked with the white number "2", was preserved in perfect condition and was additionally equipped with a radio installation – indicating that the aircraft was intended for squadron or regiment command. Compared to the MiG-1, the MiG-3 had its engine moved 10 cm forward, enlarged fuel tanks, an extended radiator cover under the fuselage, as well as new wheels and landing gear covers. However, these and other changes did not improve the poor handling characteristics of the new fighter.

A captured MiG-3 in Lithuania with a hastily painted tactical number "1", most likely in yellow or red. It appears that the trim tab is also red.

The same aircraft photographed from the other side. It's worth noting the light spot on the upper part of the rudder. The same spot is visible in the same location on the previous photo. This is most likely a mark from a repaired bullet hole.

An abandoned MiG-3 with a visible ammunition belt for the 12.7 mm UBS machine gun. The aircraft was marked with the white number "7" on the tail.

The same aircraft from the other side. Noteworthy is the damaged wing and the signs of rudder repairs by mechanics (with strips of fabric applied).

After comparing both photos, we can conclude that this captured MiG-3 in Kaunas, besides having a coloured fin tip, was also marked with the number "3" on the rudder.

The MiG-3 with a radio installation and the tactical number "8" showcases structural details between the cockpit and the engine. This beautiful aircraft shared similar flaws with its predecessor, the MiG-1. Poorly balanced and difficult to pilot, it easily entered a spin. The cause of significant losses, especially during takeoff and landing, was frequent engine failures and malfunctions in the landing gear retraction mechanism.

MiGs at the base in Kaunas or possibly in Šiauliai. The photo clearly shows that the MiGs introduced into the regiments' armament received the same marking system that was used on the previous aircraft operated by these units (e.g., the I-16). On the aircraft in the background, the division of colours on the fuselage is clearly visible, resulting from the use of different paints for the metal and wooden parts.

A MiG-3 captured by the Germans in Šiauliai. Designed as a high-altitude fighter, the MiG had its best performance at high altitudes – above 6,000 meters. However, at low altitudes, where most of the combat took place, it was sluggish and lacked manoeuvrability. German pilots observed that during low-altitude air battles, MiGs would easily enter a spin and crash.

A *Luftwaffe* soldier inspects the armament compartment of a MiG-3 captured in Kaunas. The aircraft was equipped with only two 7.62 mm ShKAS machine guns and one 12.7 mm UBS, which was entirely inadequate for air combat. Additionally, a faulty synchronizer often caused the propeller blades to be shot through, sometimes resulting in a catastrophic crash.

To increase firepower, a few fighters were equipped with two additional 12.7 mm UBK machine guns mounted under the wings. However, this installation weighed over 160 kg, significantly worsening performance and, most notably, the aircraft's manoeuvrability. In a photo likely taken in Minsk, a gondola for an additional 12.7 mm machine gun can be seen mounted under the left wing of the MiG. Aircraft equipped in this way were usually designated as MiG-3P and were most frequently used for ground attack missions.

Another MiG-3 captured in Kaunas being inspected by the Germans. This aircraft, also known from other photos, was marked on the rudder with a red number "14" outlined in white.

A similarly marked MiG-3, this time with the number "5". Kaunas airfield, summer 1941. In the background, there are I-16 aircraft.

Some MiG-3s were also equipped with bomb racks, capable of carrying up to 200 kg of bombs. These racks are clearly visible on this example captured in Kaunas, marked with the yellow number "4".

A MiG-3 in very good condition, marked with a white number "10", which was stenciled on.

The wreck of a MiG with clearly visible details of the lower part of the engine and the area where the outer wing sections were attached. Noteworthy is the large star painted on the fuselage.

One of the MiG-3s captured by the Germans at the beginning of the war. Many of these aircraft were left behind by the Soviets on airfields because they lacked trained pilots. The remaining pilots preferred to "evacuate" to the east in the familiar I-16 or I-153 aircraft rather than the difficult-to-fly MiG-3. In the regiments of the 9th SAD stationed in the occupied Polish territories, which in June 1941 had 31 MiG-1s and 201 MiG-3s, only 61 pilots had been trained on the new aircraft by the time the war broke out.

A German pilot sits in the cockpit of a MiG-3 for a commemorative photo. It's worth noting the differences in the colouration of the outer wing sections and the fuselage. They were painted in the same colour but with a different type of paint.

Photos of MiG-3 aircraft wrecks reveal many interesting elements of their construction.

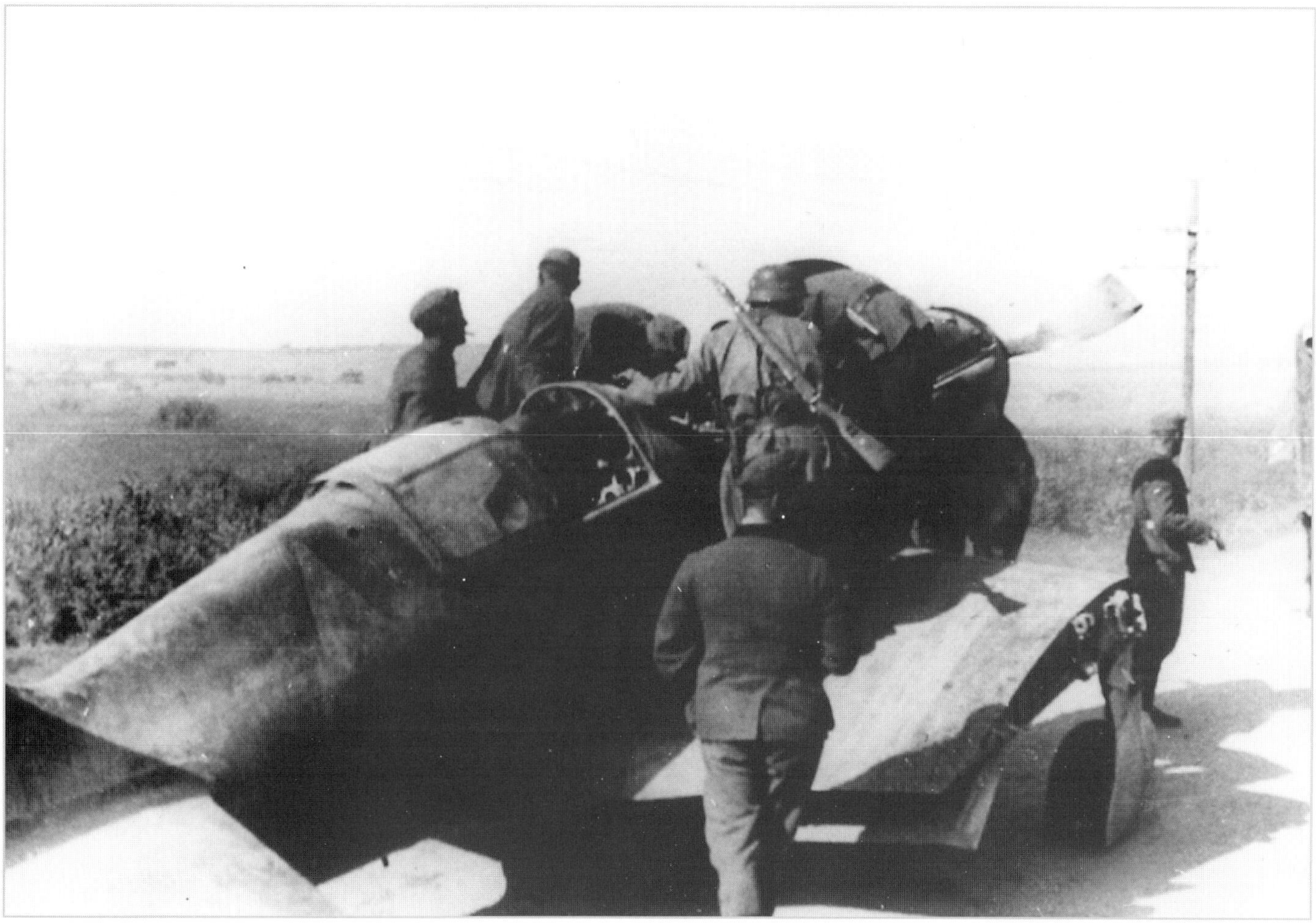

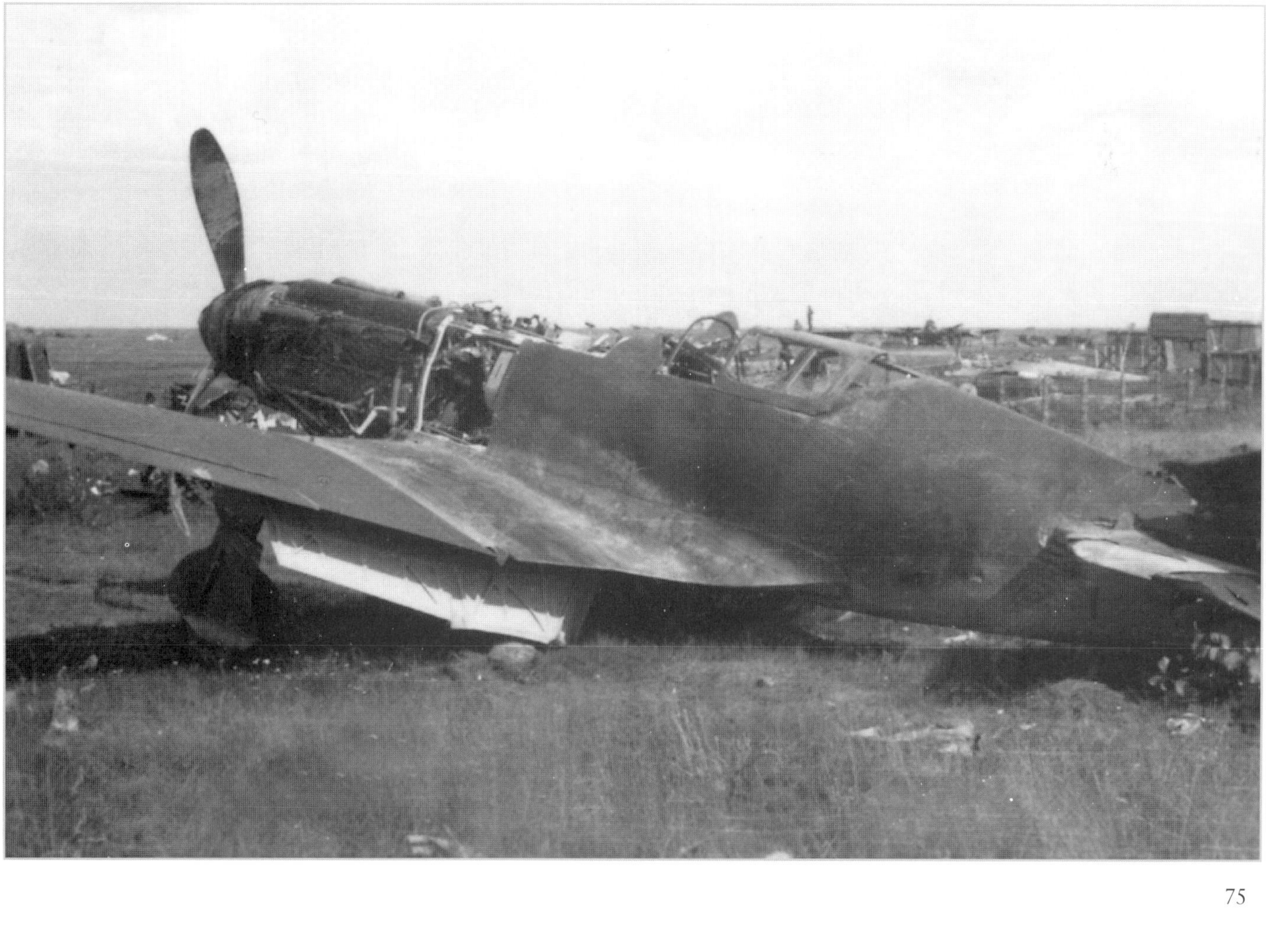

This MiG-3 was captured at the former Polish airfield Skniłów in Lwów and likely belonged to one of the regiments of the 15th SAD. Photo by Oesel.

The wreck of a MiG captured by Romanian troops on the southern front. The photo was taken in Beriozovice on 12 August 1941.

A MiG-3 equipped with a radio installation after a forced landing.

A low-quality but interesting photo showing a MiG-3 being tested by the Germans. The marking on the fuselage can be read as 6+1, which might suggest the designation I-61, as the Germans often identified this aircraft.

A camouflaged MiG-3 photographed shortly after being discovered by the Germans and a bit later – already missing some parts of its covering. Under the cockpit, there's a Russian inscription reading "For the Motherland". The design flaws of the MiG were decisive in the decision to cease its production, which was made as early as October 1941.

A group of MiG-3 aircraft captured at the airfield in Kaunas, Lithuania.

A damaged and abandoned MiG-3 left by the Soviets. It's worth noting the air intake below the exhaust pipes, the landing gear, and the removed panels in front of the cockpit.

# Lavochkin Gorbunov Gudkov LaGG-3

In addition to the MiG-3, the Soviets also launched the production of the LaGG-3 aircraft, and by the end of June 1941, they had produced 322 fighters of this type. Due to numerous flaws, the aircraft did not meet the expectations placed upon it. Nevertheless, it was modernized and produced until September 1943. At the outbreak of the war with Germany, most LaGG-3s were located in military districts in the Far East. In the European part of the USSR, only the Moscow PVO units had 75 of these aircraft, and the Leningrad Military District had 2. The LaGG-3s appeared in greater numbers on the anti-German front in the late summer and autumn of 1941.
The photo above shows a shot-down early-series LaGG-3. Notable is the dual numbering – under the pilot's cockpit and on the tail.

A shot-down later-series LaGG-3 in winter camouflage.